**FOREWORD BY
DR. SPENCER DUNCAN**

Manifesting your DESTINY

~ SECOND EDITION ~

BENJAMIN KPODO

Manifesting your
DESTINY

MnM CONCEPTS

MANIFESTING YOUR DESTINY

For further information contact
Tel: +233 24 470 9781
Email: ben_kpodo@yahoo.co.uk

Designed and Printed by
MnM Concepts, Accra-Ghana
Tel: +233 24 472 1343 | +233 50 660 0388
Email: studio.mnmconcepts@gmail.com

DEDICATION

To my late sister Augusta, who set me on the journey of my destiny. Always remembered.

FOREWORD

The question of DESTINY has loomed in the minds of many people without finding any meaningful solution.

The author has painstakingly, explained in this book the difference between the dictionary and divine definitions of the word DESTINY.

He encourages his readers to believe that God's desire is to give them all a good expected end or destiny.

To quote from the author's prescription: "this book aims at providing the panacea to any of such malady (of wrong conception of destiny) and its traces in your life. It will consume any cancer of backward, primitive and vernacular ideology, idiosyncrasy and every negative disposition of your life."

The author calls his readers to discover God's plans for their lives while stressing the fact that there are no short cuts in life and nothing happens suddenly.

He, finally, throws a challenge to the reader to begin his/her journey into greater heights by having a positive mentality; a right confession; and being disciplined and diligent in life.

Trade-in, therefore, your life of discouragement with a life of fulfilment in God's destiny as you read this superb book of MANIFESTING YOUR DESTINY.

Dr. Spencer Duncan
Haggai Institute
Singapore and Hawaii

ENDORSEMENTS

Peppered with uncommon common sense, Manifesting Your Destiny is a guide to the life we were meant to live. Drawing from dozens of sources, Benjamin's own wisdom shines through with stroke-like inspiration and encouragement. The concept of our destiny intrigues everyone, even though many will rather escape the responsibility of owning their future. We know we are gifted; we know we are created for more than adequacy; we know every day brings an opportunity for service and growth. But what we may fail to grasp is the power to shape tomorrow. The formula is true P−B−D; Perception yields Behaviour and Behaviour yields Destiny.

As you read these pages, pay attention to the words, but more importantly use their potential. Perceive the possibilities of your better future, and then act on the impulses inspired by your renewed vision. Don't settle for *'corpe diem'* (seize today). Rather *'corpe manara'* *(seize tomorrow)*!

Dr. David Schroeder
President, Pillar College,
New Jersey, USA

By a combination of poignant examples, academic excellence and spiritual depth, this book systematically brings out very clearly, simple and practical steps to helping the reader live his/her footprints in the sands of time.

Rev. Fitzgerald Odonkor
General Overseer – Harvest Chapel International

An inspiring message for our time. A must read for every young person who desires to make a mark in his/her generation. Its insight will enlighten you and the truth revealed provoke you to manifest your destiny.

John Gordon Egyir-Croffet
Director - Counselling and
Placement Centre, University of Ghana and
Director - Excellent Youth Outreach

INTRODUCTION

In life no one deliberately sets out to fail. No one plans to become a failure. Nonetheless, failure is more common than success. Success remains elusive and a mirage for many.

Many have done a lot of things in the quest to succeed. They have attended schools, attempted businesses and pursued careers but could not succeed at any of them. In their contemplation, they find various reasons for their inability to succeed.

Some have come to the sad conclusion that, that is how they have been created. They have been made and programmed to fail. Therefore, no effort of theirs will amount to anything. Nothing can change the negative omen in their favour. Forces above and beyond their domain are controlling their life. Their lot of poverty, disease, pain and misery has been determined even before they were born. That is their fate and destiny.

This perception has become so entrenched in our society that people raise their hands in despair and accept whatever comes their way. Things that could have been checked and corrected are left to rot. Diseases, which could be cured, have killed many people due to this negative mindset.

Many philosophical studies have been carried on the topic of fate or destiny, but they offer very little help in man's quest to break the shackles of backwardness and poverty; and move into the place of fulfilment. If we want to do something about our life and live in fulfilment, then we must redefine the word destiny. Indeed, we must define our own destiny and manifest it!

Manifesting Your Destiny gives a definition of the word destiny in the light of the originator of life and how to bring it to pass, fulfil it and manifest it.

Your destiny is the purpose, plan and design for your life. It is the ultimate in your life. It is all the good things that you can imagine. It is not evil but peace, joy, happiness and blessings.

It is important for everyone to know his destiny in order to be focused and purposeful in life. After this feat is achieved one must take steps to manifest it.

There are certain steps which when taken, will lead anyone into his destiny. These are ingredients needed to prepare your destiny. These are principles governed by rules and regulations, provided by Providence, to be used to manifest one's destiny.

Many have died and were buried with great gifts and talents. They died poor and weak while they had what it took to change the course of history. A lot of people have left this world without a memorial. This is because they failed to manifest their destinies.

This book aims at providing the panacea to any such malady and its traces in your life. I believe the information in this book will consume any cancer of backward, primitive and vernacular ideology, idiosyncrasy and every negative disposition of your life. It is my sincere desire to see changes of improvement in your life and that of many others. If you want a transformation, journey with me through the pages of this book.

You can live in fulfilment. You can find your name in the world's hall of fame, if you resolve to manifest your destiny today by reading this book.

TABLE OF CONTENTS

*To believe success,
wealth and prosperity
belong to a chosen
few is a lie.*

Chapter One

THERE IS A PLAN FOR YOUR LIFE

I was at the crossroad of life;
Not knowing where to turn.
I waited and waited but there was none.
None to show the way;
That leads to my destiny.
Then I saw the Lord.
I wanted to ask,
Lord; 'show me the way to my destiny'.
But before I could ask,
He said, 'follow me'.
I followed obediently;
Though I knew not where He was leading me.
We walked silently,
Meeting neither man nor beast.
'What a lonely way' said my heart.
Then in a moment I saw it!
Hidden all along from me is a glorious place!
Then He said; 'son you're the one to traverse this road,

Well done!
Behold your destination!
Behold your destiny!'

The destiny of everyone is the end or destination of his life. It is the climax of the person's life. It is the highest point of glory you can attain in life. Your destiny is fulfilling your God given agenda on this earth.

Before you read any further, I want you to know and understand that every man or woman including you has a God-given purpose and agenda, a destiny. Under no circumstance whatsoever should you confuse this divine design and purpose with the world's notion of destiny. The Dictionary renders destiny as fate; that which cannot be changed by any effort and is bound to happen no matter what you do about it. It is the inevitable good or evil. It cannot be changed, prevented or stopped no matter the effort applied.

Various definitions equate it to the ideology of fatalism. This has made many who believe their efforts today can affect their fortunes tomorrow in one way or the other to shudder at the mention of the word and have therefore wiped it out of their vocabulary.

The above meaning of the word destiny has made many people accept whatever comes their way. They have come to believe that no effort of theirs can change their situations. The odds are against them and the omen is not in their favour. Millions are suffering due to this negative mind set. They are living in pain, misery, poverty and sickness and somehow, rather strangely they see it as 'normal'. They do nothing to change their situation. To them, that is how God made and designed them to be. That is their destiny. How sad!

The belief that man is the architect of his own life without the help and guidance of God is the sin of pride. It is the error of the new age and the madness of enlightenment. On the other hand, the belief that everything that happens to man is done by God regardless of his effort is the sin of fatalism. It is the shackle of backwardness and the prison of mediocrity.

To believe success, wealth and prosperity belong to a chosen few is a lie. No one is destined or sentenced to live in pain and misery. All humans are created equal, with the necessary potential for success. Thus, the destiny of everyone is good. Its fulfilment is to bring joy and happiness and make the world a better place. To believe otherwise is real bondage! And I pray you be delivered from every negative mindset and such bondage!

Your lot is better than what you have now; you are designed for greater heights. You are not a chicken; you are an eagle and you do not belong to the ground. Your dwelling is high above where the eagles fly. Begin to see your destiny the way God sees it and be not limited by the status quo and by the lies peddled by the devil. Free yourself from every entanglement and web of deception. You were not made to suffer shame and disgrace. You were born to live!

Jesus said:

> *"But I am come that ye might have life and have it more abundantly." - **John 10:10b***

The saviour came that you should live and not just live but to abound and excel in living; that you should live more abundantly. It means living out your destiny. Your inferior state is the devil's design. Satan is the architect of evil. He is evil and he loves unleashing evil on mankind. Right from the beginning of creation he sought to distort God's destiny for mankind.

> *"The devil came not but to steal, kill and destroy!"*
> *- **John10:10a***

The devil's work has been to steal, kill and to destroy. It is sad to say the devil has succeeded in stealing the destinies of many, killed and destroyed them. Blessed one, do not allow the devil to come near your life and destiny, he will steal both and see to it that they are destroyed.

Christ came to restore your life and destiny. He came to reverse the trend. He came to destroy the devil and to give you life and purpose for living. By His redemptive work on the cross, the works of the devil were destroyed.

> *"For this purpose the son of man was manifested, that he might destroy the works of the devil." -*
> *1 John 3:8b*

Friend, the backwardness in many parts of the world has its source or roots in wrong belief. Many are they that walk on the streets and do not see any bright future. To them there is nothing wrong with the high unemployment levels, low-income levels, high illiteracy rate, and low output levels. It is no wonder to come across people in the pursuit of knowledge in universities and other higher institutions of learning who are afflicted by the same malady. To them, the squalor and poverty is *'normal'* because it is determined by forces that we cannot control or manipulate.

We have been unable to tame our land. How on earth could anyone limit his capacity and ability to improve and progress as we have sadly done? We throw our hands in the air and blame our sad state on forces beyond our control.

It is shameful and disgraceful to our nature as human beings, created by God and having His very essence or nature to live a life of failure, non-achievement and non-attainment. When God created you, He filled you with His own breath, the active force that enables you to continue His creation. God has deposited in you every potential needed to make life worth living and living well.

> *"According as his divine power hath given unto us all things that pertain unto life and godliness through the knowledge of him that hath called us to glory and virtue." - **2 Peter 1:3***

The picture of backwardness portrayed all around is not what God intends for mankind. The destiny I am talking about is your future and destination in the sight of God.

The Bible says:

> *"And there is hope in thine end saith the Lord." - **Jeremiah 31:17***

This is the word of the Lord to anybody who puts his trust in Him and acknowledges the Lord in his heart and life. The word says; *'there is hope in thine end'*. Hope is the positive anticipation one has regarding the future. We hope for good things that will bring us joy and happiness. When we say something is beyond hope, it means there is no indication whatsoever that it will prosper or ever succeed. Your end is your destiny in the sight of God, which is nothing but good. Your story is not beyond hope.

It is said; *'tomorrow never comes'*, but believe me, your tomorrow shall come, because God says so. Nothing, no man, woman or devil can stop you from seeing and enjoying your tomorrow, and your destiny because God said so, it shall come to pass.

Dear one, surely *'there is hope in thine end'*. Your destiny is that of success and not failure, happiness and not sadness, peace and tranquillity and not strife, wealth and not poverty, laughter and not weeping, joy and not mourning. I say with conviction. *'There is hope in thine end!'*

The good Lord does not intend that you suffer pain, hardship and misery, or that your life is characterized by difficulties permanently. The negativity that surrounds you is not of God. Never resign to fate. Never should you give up. Never accept the situation the way it is. No!

"God did not create you to live on the sidelines, but to win the game." - **Dale Galloway**

Do not live on the side-lines! You are not meant to be a mere spectator. Wear your boots, pull up your socks and get on the pitch. You are qualified to be on the pitch. Get into the game for victory is assured!

The scripture says:

"For I know the thoughts I think towards you, saith the Lord, thoughts of peace and not evil to give you an expected end." - Jeremiah 29:11

Read the above quotation again; imagine the words, how unique! The thoughts of God towards you are thoughts of peace and not evil. Why? To give you an expected end, a destiny.

This is the word of God spoken by the prophet Jeremiah to the people of Israel, who were being held in captivity in Babylon. In their affliction, God said His thought towards them was to give them an expected end. This was the time that the people of God were in captivity. They were slaves in a strange land. They were subjected to a dehumanising situation. The city of the Lord had been destroyed. Jerusalem had been burnt down and its walls had been broken down. The temple of the Lord had been burnt with fire and the precious things of the temple had been carried away. The land of Israel was desolate. Yet God said there was an expected end for them. Their destiny as a chosen nation was still glorious.

The life you are going through may not be the best. Your situation may be so dire and serious. Your circumstances may be so precarious, but I have news for you! God is fervently thinking and planning an expected end for you. A victorious glorious end. It is not over yet, friend, cheer up; the game is not over.

Destiny is a divine subject. Its fulfilment is based on Gods principles. Nevertheless, it does not mean God will manifest your destiny without your involvement. God works through your circumstances and with your abilities to bring about your destiny. And the wonderful consolation is that it is always good and not evil.

Your destiny is not evil; it is not poverty, sickness, pain, sorrow and trouble. It is not to bring you tears and gnashing of teeth. Rather, it is wealth, health, joy, happiness and peace. It is to bring fulfilment and to make you a blessing unto humanity.

It is important to emphasise that destiny is the divine plan for mankind. It is God's plan and design for you; it is the reason for which He made you. Your destiny is like a plan and a design; it must therefore be uncovered and understood before it can be accomplished. It is like an architectural edifice, which cannot be put up without a careful study of the drawings and a plan.

It is imperative to know your destiny if you want to manifest it and live in fulfilment.

*The greatest disease
in the world is ignorance;
it has caused more damage
than any disease.*

Chapter Two

KNOWING THE PLAN FOR YOUR LIFE

It is said; *'knowledge is power'*, the active energy for production. Without it, resources are wasted. It is only after you have acquired the necessary knowledge of a phenomenon that you can apply it for your own good.

All the laws of science existed before they were discovered. However, the usefulness of any law is not based on its existence. Rather it is based on its discovery. The law of aerodynamics became useful and has been used to amazing degrees after it was discovered.

All the minerals existed in the earth crust for generations, but it did not profit our forefathers because they did not know what they were, let alone know their use. It has been said, hundreds of years ago diamonds were used to kill birds in Southern Africa, because its worth and importance was not known.

Knowledge brings liberty, illumination and peace of mind. When you have knowledge you are in control, you are in charge and you are above.

Friend, any prison you find yourself in today, whether it is financial, spiritual or social will become unable to hold you if you acquire the needed knowledge concerning its dynamics.

Knowing your destiny is very important and it is an imperative if you ever want to be what God made you to be and to become a blessing to many.

> *"Through wisdom is an house built; and by understanding it is established.*
>
> *And by knowledge shall the chambers be filled with all precious and pleasant riches."- **Proverbs 24: 3-4**

It remains true that by knowledge the chambers are filled with all precious and pleasant riches. Without knowledge your life becomes empty and void. Knowledge indeed adds colour to your life and makes your life beautiful.

According **Victor E. Frankl,** a neurologist and psychiatrist; as well as a holocaust survivor

> *"Life expects something of you, and it is up to every individual to discover what it should be."*

You can only become what you have knowledge of, dream of, think of, see and hope to be. Your problem of failure is half solved if you know the purpose for which you were created. No athlete runs a race without knowing how long the race will take. Life in many instances is like a race; hence you cannot run it without being aware of its end. Your destiny is the ultimate of your life, knowing it keeps you in focus. You do not beat about the bush or run aimlessly.

The psalmist said:

> *"They know not, neither will they understand; they walk on in darkness; all the foundations of the earth are out of course.*
>
> *I have said, Ye are gods; and all of you are children of the Most High.*
>
> *But Ye shall die like men, and fall like one of the princes." - **Psalm 82: 5-7***

Dear one, do not die like a mere man. Mere men are killed by ignorance. You are worth far more than you think of yourself. The law of reproduction says, *'like father like son'* or *'like mother like daughter'*. My people say, *'the child of the tilapia does not look like a catfish'*. You are a child of God, the greatest king. You are a prince or princess of a royal priesthood, a peculiar person and a chosen one. You cannot be destined to be failure.

Hellen Keller was born blind, deaf and dumb but she rose up above her impossible condition. She became an author, a political activist and conference speaker. She was also the first deaf and blind person to earn a Bachelor of Arts degree.

She said;

> *"Worse than being blind would be to be able to see but not have any vision."* - **Helen Keller**

It is a pity to come across men well advanced in years, who do not know what their existence in this world is for? They eat, drink, sleep and do whatever comes their way without any sense of purpose. Friend, this is a tragedy that should not happen. Such people are lazy, not diligent and careless. They live aimlessly and it does not matter how long they live. They remain non-achievers and failures. They die with their destiny intact, well ahead of them. Because they fail to recognise it.

> *"Where there is no vision the people perish."*
> - **Proverbs 29:18a**

Vision is simply the knowledge of what should be done. It is the desired end which you have set your mind on. It is the good you want to achieve. Once it is clear, your efforts are directed towards fulfilling it.

"A vision is the guidepost that keeps you on track with God's plan for your life." - **Kevin Baerg**

An individual or a people without a vision will surely perish. A church without a vision is bedevilled with strife and contention. Such a church has no future. Any enterprise without a vision is doomed, it will die a slow and painful death. If there is no vision, there will be no destiny and life will be reduced to a game of chance, a dangerous game of survival.

"With good vision you not only see with your eyes but your heart." - **Zig Ziglar**

The importance of knowing your destiny cannot be over emphasised but the million-dollar question is how do I know my destiny? How do I know what the Lord wants me to do and achieve in this life? What am I really made for?

REMOVE THE CURTAIN

It is only when you have your destiny in sight, that you can manifest it. However, the challenge is that many cannot see well, they have a problem with their vision. There is something obstructing their view. A curtain seems to be denying them the privilege of seeing the world in its true colours.

Remove the curtain and your success will be staring at you in the face, all you will need to do is to reach it and grab it.

I penned the short poem below to illustrate the importance of prayer in removing the curtain no matter the material it is made of.

Prayer is the force
That moves mountains
Lowers the hills
Exalts the valleys
The man that learns to use it
Possesses a powerful instrument
That paves his way.

Prayer is a potent weapon and it will remove any curtain that obstructs your view. You can have a full view of your destiny through prayer. It is the one who manufactured an object that knows how best it can operate, what it is designed for and what it is not fashioned for. Prayer links you with God your maker. And by it your destiny is revealed to you. You must pray diligently to uncover your purpose on this earth. Remove the fog and the darkness by the power of prayer. Then you will have your way and see clearly.

God intends everyone to be fulfilled in life. However, the adversary always works to prevent God's design from coming to pass. The enemy work is to ensure you do not know your destiny; he tries to keep your eyes off it. And so long as you are not in the know, there is no way you will become an achiever. You will lack the power to drive you forward. Remember, *'knowledge is power'*!

Sometimes you must battle with the forces of darkness to have your goal in sight. To everyone the devil assigns a *'strongman'* that works to deprogram the program of God for his life. This *'strongman'* works twenty-four hours a day to ensure your failure.

But thank God for Jesus, who

> *"Having spoiled principalities and powers he made a show of them openly, triumphing over them in it."*
> *- Colossians 2:15*

And, He is seated far above all principalities and powers. You have what it takes to paralyse and destroy every strongman assigned against your life. In prayer you bind every power fighting against your life. If things are so complicated and there is no clarity, please engage in serious prayer. We call it warfare prayer. Where you make known your position in the Lord and forcefully resit the devil. As you engage in such prayers, the devil will have no option but to pack bag and baggage and leave you in peace.

> *"For we wrestle not against flesh and blood, but against principalities, against powers, against rulers of the darkness of this world, against spiritual wickedness in high places." - **Ephesians 6:12***

There is also the need to pray that your desires and ambitions fall in line with the will of God for your life. If your ambitions are miles away from the purpose of God for your life, manifesting your destiny becomes a mirage. This prayer is called total surrender to the Lord.

Friend! Surrender everything and ask the Lord to take control and do His will in your life. Ask the Lord to keep you on His path so that you do not deviate neither to the left nor to the right.

DROP THE SCALES

The man that gives himself to study improves himself, maintains his course, fulfils his mission and becomes useful to mankind.

He that is prepared to learn will surely be great.

The present generation is given to too much frivolity; there is no time for study. Books remain on the shelves and gather dust. Certainly, the best way to improve your lot is through study. Buy books, develop an interest in reading and you will see yourself becoming a better person than you use to be.

On the eve of the day Kofi Annan, the former United Nations Secretary General received his Nobel Peace Prize, he granted an interview wherein he mentioned reading as one of the things he engages in at his leisure times. No wonder he was respected for his insight and understanding.

There is no darkness but ignorance
Knowledge is light
Ignorance is darkness
Get knowledge and light will
Shine in your darkness
And ignorance will be far from you
Then, the scales will drop off from your eyes.

It is a pity to see Christians with no knowledge of the scriptures, thriving only on words that proceed from the pulpit, from men of God, some of who have little or shallow knowledge of the scriptures themselves. They misapply scriptures and give un-meditated jargons as revelations from God.

Someone said; '*A little learning is a dangerous thing*'. Strive to acquire knowledge and be a thoroughbred in your chosen field of life.

The person who has a partial knowledge of something is likely to misapply his knowledge. For instance, when a person becomes a dropout in a course he still talks and behaves as someone who has completed the course. He talks as an authority, but his information is dangerous because it is not complete.

Paul, knowing we are vulnerable to this malady provided the panacea in the letter to Timothy.

He wrote:

> "*Study to show thyself approved unto God, a workman that needed not to be ashamed rightly dividing the word of truth.*" - ***2 Timothy 2:15***

Study the word of God, for it contains the mind of God and the state of man. The word of God contains all you need to know about God and yourself. What the Bible says about you is what you are or should be. The earlier you know it the better. The word of God is your map and staff. It is also a sword and a weapon of war. Use it! Ignorance is an evil disease that is very ruthless. It destroys in silence, leaving pain and misery in its wake.

How many have died of things that should not have kill them. But their ignorance was like a death sentence, sending them to the gallows.

Indeed, the greatest disease in the world is ignorance; it has caused more damage than any disease you can think of.

Knowledge is therefore a necessity. For a man cannot be greater than what he knows.

Dear one, if you want to walk your path and fulfil your dreams and visions, I recommend you depend on the knowledge in word of God. In it lies your expansion. Begin to search the scriptures concerning YOU, your vocation and career and you will find your destiny.

To study is to improve your lot in the future. Everyone should do everything possible to get more knowledge. The world is ruled by knowledge and the more you have the larger your territory. Years of strenuous study always pay. If you are energetic, you have the advantage of your vitality to acquire a lot of information. Your years of education should be taken seriously; it is never a waste of time.

I have come across people who constantly regret their lack of seriousness when they were in school. They thought they should be allowed to do whatever seemed right to them. Today, they have realised they were very wrong. They have come so close to their success many a time but were unable to cross over because they failed to produce a proof of their knowledge which is a certificate.

These are days of information; the know-how of yesterday cannot be applied to today's problem. Look at the transformation brought about by the revolution of information technology in our days. Anyone who refuses to catch up is left behind. It does not matter your field of operation; with additional information you are bound to go forward.

The truth shall set you free says the scriptures. However, it is the truth you know that will set you free and not the truth just by itself. In the truth lies the power to set you free and liberate you but until you know it, it remains a passive power that is not activated to help you.

One area where we fail in knowledge is when it comes to ourselves. We fail miserably to study the reason why we are alive, the reason why we were created. You must do an introspection of your life, to know your strengths and your weaknesses, to know your abilities and talents. Every man is created with certain endowments that give him a distinct destiny. The businesspeople call it competitive advantage. These endowments set him apart and allows him to be an originator and not a carbon copy.

Thousands of years ago Socrates, one of the greatest ancient Greek Philosophers made this statement *'Man, know thyself'*. Today, after so many years we still find it difficult to do as he said.

Drop the scales off your eyes by acquiring knowledge through study. By study you will know what you are worth, what you have been created for and what your destiny is all about.

VISIONS OF THE NIGHT

Visions of the night are revelations to our soul and spirit when we lose consciousness in sleep. These are what we call dreams. Every 'normal' human being has experienced a dream before. Some are so vivid that you wake up with the experience of the dream, thinking it was real.

We tend to have dreams almost anytime we sleep. It is a form of sub-conscious imagination. This form of imagination is largely not hindered by the prevailing conditions you are experiencing, because you are not conscious of your environment when you sleep, so your mind is devoid of the negativity that you may be experiencing.

In most cases dreams become wakeful experiences. Thus, there has been a lot of attempts to interpret dreams by various people. Some have tried to categorize them and given varied interpretation to them. However, every dream a person dreams carries specific information and cannot and should not be interpreted based on that of another person.

Let me caution that some dreams carry no information. The Bible says they are dreams we cause ourselves to dream. They are mostly an extension of our day's experience. We easily forget such dreams. However, there are dreams that we simply cannot forget. Such a dream is unforgettable, it troubles your soul and spirit and you do not feel comfortable. Even if you cannot remember it, it troubles your whole body.

Some dreams are evil and demonic. Most of these dreams are horrifying encounters, which we call nightmares. To prevent evil and demonic dreams in your life, you should severe yourself from anything that links you to the devil. Live a pure and a holy life and eschew evil.

Be like Joseph, be righteous and God shall reveal your destiny to you in a vision of the night.

Many have had dreams that have been a vivid representation of their own destiny, the destiny of others, their families and country. Your destiny can be revealed to you in a dream. And when you apply yourself to manifesting it, it will surely come to pass.

Joseph had a dream that spelt out his destiny. In the passage of time it became a reality.

> *"And Joseph dreamed a dream, and he told it to his brethren: and they hated him yet the more.*
>
> *And he said unto them, hear I pray you, this dream which I have dreamed:*
>
> *For, behold we were binding sheaves in the field, and lo, my sheaf arose, and stood upright; and, behold, your sheaves stood round about, and made obeisance to my sheaf...*
>
> *And he dream yet another dream, and told it to his brethren, and said, Behold, I have dreamed a dream more; behold the sun and the moon and the eleven stars made obeisance to me." - **Genesis 37:5-9***

Joseph's brothers hated him for his dreams, which suggested that he was going to be lord over them. However, Jacob the father being a prophet understood the dreams and observed them. He waited for their manifestation. And we all know Joseph's dreams became a reality.

PROPHETIC WORD

By a prophetic word you can also get to know your destiny. This is the plan of God concerning your life revealed to you by a man of God. It could take the form of a prophecy, where the spirit of God speaks through his servant or by a vision shown to him about you. It could even be to you personally. A prophetic word could also be a scripture in the Bible, which becomes a rhema - spoken word – to you. It is like it was written just for you.

In these last days, there has been a lot of emphasis on the prophetic ministry. This is because the prophet Joel said in the last days the young ones shall prophecy. Many claims to have this spiritual gift. You find men with the title, prophet all over.

Although this is a good development, it has been marred by the over emphasis placed on it by many. The revered *thus sayest the Lord* is no longer taken seriously. Nonetheless, prophecy plays a major role in the final move of God. It will herald the great harvest of the Lord. Many lives have been turned around as a proof of the importance of this gift of the spirit.

What determines the validity of a prophecy is its outcome. If it is from God it will surely come to pass, if its conditions are fulfilled. Many of the prophecies in the Bible are now being fulfilled after many years.

> *"Believe in the Lord your God, so shall ye be established; believe his prophets, so shall ye prosper." - 2 Chronicles 20:20b*

In the scripture, there are so many instances of the prophetic word. In the book of Luke, Chapter One, the angel Gabriel brought a prophetic word to the Virgin Mary, and all that the angel said came to pass. What is it that has been said concerning you? Believe it, work at it, if it is from God, though it tarries, it shall not tarry. It will come to fruition.

Personal Conviction

In knowing your destiny, the last thing, I would like to talk about is what I call personal conviction.

Nobody should cause you to do that which you should not do. Your conviction is the check to prevent you from following wild and demonic dreams and lies peddled in the name of God. God has put in you His spirit to lead you into glory and honour. You can get to know your destiny by your convictions. Conviction means a strong belief or opinion of something. When you are convinced about something, it gives you peace of mind.

There are certain careers you should not pursue no matter the financial reward because there is something in you that tells you, this is not what you have been made for. You simply should not do them because it will bring you no satisfaction, joy and fulfilment

Check the things you are inclined to do naturally. What are your hobbies? What do you normally do at your free time? What are your favourite subjects? These could be signals to your destiny.

There are hardly any logical reasons for the likes or dislikes of a person. It is just a matter of disposition. An indication of the person's assignment and purpose.

When you purge your mind from sin, by renewing it with the word of God, you are developing a good conscience. A good conscience is needed if you want your convictions to be your guide. Without a good conscience your conviction will lead you into destruction. When you are at peace with God, He orders your steps. You can go ahead and follow your own leading.

You cannot determine if you will dream or not. Neither can you determine when you will receive a word of prophecy. You cannot force or manipulate a prophet to prophecy to you. If you try you will be deceived. However, if you develop your conscience, your convictions become the surest guide and check on your life.

It is wonderful how this personal conviction works. For example, there are business ventures you enter into and immediately you realise there is something wrong about the whole venture. If you have over the years trained your conscience you will not take certain steps. Even the word of prophecy must agree with your conviction, otherwise you may be led astray by lies peddled in the name of God.

Child of God, believe your convictions, they will lead you into your destiny.

When your destiny is in sight then you can reach it and manifest it.

*Do not be deceived;
everything is a result
of a process. Without the
process there will be
no product.*

Chapter Three

NO SUDDEN FLIGHT

The greatest achievement in life is to manifest your destiny, to become what you were created for, to live in fulfilment and to become a blessing. The whole of this book is about helping you accomplish this high goal in life and to show forth your destiny.

In the proceeding chapters, I have provided the ingredients needed to prepare the meal of your destiny, steps that lead to your destination. These are principles of God that remain valid in all circumstances. They are laid down steps, which when taken will lead anyone into the realms of success. They have been tried and tested since time immemorial. They are gemstones that will turn around the life of anyone that possesses them and puts them to use.

Before we examine these ingredients one by one, it is important to know that there are no short cuts in life and that nothing happens suddenly.

It is said,

"The height that great men reached and attained was not gotten by a sudden flight. But they while their companions slept were toiling upwards."

There is no magic wand! The man who wakes up to find himself great, has not been asleep. Manifesting your destiny does not take a sudden flight, but rather it takes a consciously ordered approach. I want you to get the right perception. It is a sin for you to think God will take you into your Promised Land without any effort from you. You must do the walking, the crossing of the sea and river, the climbing and descending of the mountains, the driving away of the enemy, the fighting and the possessing of the land.

"There's no easy path to glory, there's no rosy path to fame...!" - **Unknown**

In life there are no easy roads. Nothing of value is gotten on a silver platter. The maxim goes, *'no lasting glory is won without struggle'*. Manifesting means showing forth and bringing to light. The Oxford Advanced Learners Dictionary defines manifest as *'showing clearly'*. The purpose of this book is to put you in a position where you can easily attain and exhibit your destiny.

When you read the account of the day of Pentecost in the book of Acts Chapter Two, you are told of the sudden baptism of the Holy Ghost. The event was sudden but wait a little. The disciples had been gathered in the upper room for days. Nothing happened when they begun but they kept on praying and suddenly the purpose of their gathering was fulfilled. If they had stopped after the first day nothing would have been heard of them again.

Do not be deceived, everything is as a result of a process. Without the process there will be no product. Beware; there are no sudden flights, no easy path to glory and no fulfilment of prophecy without the waging of a good warfare.

Some people do not eat meat because of the process the animal goes through before it is put on the table. They cannot stand the slaughtering and processing of it. The process may not be nice, it may not be attractive, but it remains the only way the product is arrived at. You may have resolved to take fish in place of meat, but you may be shocked the way fish is handled either.

Whenever I see a vessel of clay, I see a lump of clay that has gone through a lot of processes. The vessel was not dug out of the earth. In the same way, like clay we must undergo the processes of life to manifest our destiny.

Christianity is not about us expecting God to do everything for us. It is about us doing the works of God. And becoming a blessing unto our generation.

What is the use of the rains if the grounds are not prepared for it? Do not put your hands in your bosom. Nothing is achieved by that method.

Manifesting your destiny is a very important undertaking; you should engage yourself in, in order to live a fulfilled life on this earth. In your destiny lie your peace, prosperity and happiness. Without its manifestation, life becomes an endless battle for survival. You are not yet successful until you have fulfilled your destiny. Generations yet unborn are counting on you. Your success is the success of many that are looking up to you. You should not fail them. Posterity will not forgive you if you disappoint your generation. You must therefore manifest your purpose and destiny in your age and dispensation.

*"For the earnest expectation of the creation waiteth for the manifestation of the sons of God." - **Romans 8:19***

Everything is waiting for your showing forth.

Nevertheless, reaching your destiny involves sweat and blood. The truth is that there are so many things God has put in place for us, but we must fight for them. Remember the land flowing with milk and honey was not reached on the spur of the moment. Rather, it took a gradual walk over sand and rock.

*"Concerning all acts
of initiative and creation,
there is one elementary
truth- that the moment one
definitely commits oneself,
then providence moves too."*

- Goethe -

Chapter Four

GET STARTED

Every achiever has a beginning. Nobody wakes up to find himself great. Every building has a foundation. You must also begin somewhere. It is in starting a project that it can be completed. Without a beginning there can be no end. The only time you have available to make or unmake your life is today.

Now that you have your destiny in sight, now that you are convinced about what your life is meant for, all that you need to do is to plunge into it. Jump into the water; for it is only in the water that you learn how to swim. No one learns how to drive a car with a motor bicycle. It is in doing that we learn how it can be done and done well.

If you remain at the junction of your destiny and keep looking at the direction of your destiny, thinking some wind will come and blow you along, then you will be there till the sun goes down.

Lao Tzu the great Chinese philosopher and older contemporary of Confucius said,

"The journey of a thousand miles begins with a step."

Friend, he that takes steps remains not at the same place. He shall certainly go forward. Also, you should remember that every assignment has a time period in which it should be executed, the earlier it is done the better. It is in going forward that the finish line is crossed.

Below is a valuable counsel:

"First, do not begin anything that has not been thought out from all aspects and recognized as possessing a permanent and relatively high value.

*Second, he will be successful who starts the execution as soon as practicable after the choice. Thus, not the hasty start but the decided and the early beginning is of value. Hesitation and delay are to be discouraged as non-values." - **Johann Lindworsky***

The man who keeps postponing what he ought to do will not succeed, because procrastination is the thief of time and time wasted cannot be retrieved. Time is the most important asset a person has. It is the greatest tool of the youth, but sadly many just sit and allow the most productive part of their lives to go waste. They grow up full of regret and sorrow. They refused to make hay while the sun was shining and forgot that a stitch in time saves nine.

Paul of Tarsus, the apostle wrote to the church of Ephesus,

> *"Wherefore, he saith Awake thou that sleepest, and arise from the dead and Christ shall give thee light.*
>
> *See, then, that ye walk circumspectly, not as fools but as wise,*
>
> *Redeeming the time because the days are evil."* **Ephesians 5:14-16**

When a man keeps postponing the time, he will bath in a day he may end up sleeping without bathing. **Having a great idea without doing anything about it amounts to nothing.** No matter how nice the story you have in your head, no one will appreciate it, if it remains untold. What use is the plan of a magnificent building if it remains on the drawing board?

> *"Everyone who's ever taken a shower has had an idea. It is the person who gets out of the shower, dries off and does something about it who makes the difference." - **Nolan Bushnell***

The world gives way to the person who has resolved to cross his river, who begins to paddle his canoe, who begins his journey no matter how long and dark the way seems. **When you know you must get something accomplished, do not wait for a better day, because there will be no better day.**

"Arise, shine for thy light is come." - ***Isaiah 60:1***

The scripture says, arise, shine because your light has already come, and it is still present. Note, the use of the comma after the word, arise. It means when you arise it follows automatically that you shine. Arise, begin, and you will succeed.

"Only begin and he mind grows heated, only begin and the task will be completed" - ***Goethe***

The right time will never come. Your goal will remain a goal if you keep waiting for the opportune time. You will remain at the junction of your destiny, if you think by some celestial means a wind will come and blow you along. No! Take the bull by the horn, begin to till your farm early and always know the early bird catches the fat worms.

Some wise man said,

> *"Procrastination attracts the lazy man and it attracts failure too."*

Take advantage of the opportunities that come your way. They are the doorways to your destiny. No matter how unfortunate you think you are, your time will surely come. Time and chance happen to all men. What matters is how prepared you are for your opportunity? Even if you have missed so many opportunities, God will bring many more your way. Take advantage of whatever the Lord brings your way. Do not sit down and let them pass.

> *"Knowing what your goal is and desiring to reach does not bring you closer to it. Doing something does."* **- George Eld**

Do not procrastinate. No one will or can manifest your destiny for you. The earlier you get this truth the better. Begin right away!

*"Whatever gains you
obtain by sinful means
become an instrument of
oppression and cruelty."*

Chapter Five

THE ROAD TO SUCCESS

There are many roads that leads to various destinations, some good and some evil. However, he that walks on the way of righteousness will surely reach the destination of success.

*"Mark the perfect man, and behold the upright; for the end of that man is peace." - **Psalm 37:37***

The righteous' end is peace. Peace here means fulfilment, prosperity and success. The person who keeps himself pure will have his destiny clearly spelled out by God and he will achieve it. Peace is the single word that sums up your destiny.

The wise man said:

*"The integrity of the upright shall guide them but the perverseness of the transgressors shall destroy them." - **Proverbs 11: 3***

The righteous shall be led into their destinies, because

their very righteousness shall guide them. Their steps are ordered. They do not get into the complications of life. Rather they live a simple but purposeful life.

Due to the perverseness of the world in these last days, righteousness has been swept under the carpet. Holy living is no longer the focus of the Christian life. Sin and immorality have become the order of the day. Even those who profess to bear the name of Christ are committing all sorts of evil.

This unholy life is becoming entrenched in our society. It is sad to come across evil in our churches. Ministers of the gospel have lost sight of this cardinal point. Righteousness is no longer preached from the pulpit, sin is no longer exposed and given the treatment it deserves, rather it has become the norm.

This is a tragedy; we have forgotten that;

> *"Righteousness exalts a nation but sin is a reproach to any people." -* **Proverbs 14:34**

Indeed, sin is a reproach; it is like a bad label on a product. It takes away the glory of man; the very essence of mankind. There is something about sin, it takes away the joy of man and makes him weak. Sin is dangerous, it should not be entertained. When you welcome it into your life you will have to drive it away with force because it will not go by itself.

> *"A man by his sin may waste himself, which to waste that which on earth is most like God. This is man's greatest tragedy, God's heaviest grief – Sin has many sides and many ramifications. It is like a disease with numberless complications, any one of which can kill the patient." -* **A. W. Tozer**

Righteousness exalts a nation, a family and a man; it also lifts man into the glory of God and places him on the pinnacle of his destiny.

Holiness puts you in the safety of God's presence. It is a refuge and a stronghold, for as long as you remain holy and righteous, no devil will dare come near you because you enjoy the protection of the Most High. Therefore, it is necessary and binding on anyone who wants to live in fulfilment to walk in holiness.

Remember God is a righteous God and will not make Himself known unto a sinful man. When you live a holy life, your destiny comes into light, it is illuminated because,

> *"In Him we live and move and have our being." -* **Acts 17: 28**

And all that you will have to do is to reach it, grab it and manifest it.

Righteousness is a state, a place of standing in God, where you are on God's side. To be righteous is to be holy. It means to be set apart for a special use. It is to be prepared for God's use all the time. It is agreeing with God, to please Him always by doing what is right and abstaining from evil and sin. You remain in this state so long as you eschew evil and do the will of God.

The righteous man commands the host of heaven to his side. He enjoys angelic visitation because the hand of God is upon him. That is why David said he has never seen the righteous forsaken. He manifests his destiny and his children cannot beg for bread.

In these days of uncertainty and fear, courage and boldness are indispensable. To be alive and successful is to risk so many things. You therefore need courage and boldness to succeed in this life. However, these virtues are not sold in the shop across the street, they are by-products of righteousness.

*"The wicked flee when no man persueth but the righteous shall be bold as a lion." - **Proverbs 28:1***

Indeed, the road to success is righteousness. If you walk on this road you command the host of heaven to your side. Heavenly presence will always be with you on this road. You shall be fruitful all the days of your life.

> *"Blessed is the man who walketh not in the counsel of the ungodly, nor standeth in the way of sinners, nor sitteth in the seat of the scornful.*
>
> *But his delight is in the law of the Lord; and in his law doth he meditate day and night.*
>
> *And he shall be like a tree planted by the rivers of water, that bringeth forth its fruits in its season; its leaf also shall not wither; and whatsoever he doeth shall prosper". - **Psalm 1:1-3***

The Holy Scripture says; when the foundations are destroyed what will the righteous do? I believe in times of difficulty, the righteous have a way out. When the foundations are destroyed the righteous just hang onto the Lord.

Without holiness humans will go all lengths in the name of success. Whatever gains you obtain by sinful means become an instrument of oppression and cruelty. In fact, it does not benefit anyone. True success is achieved in the light of God. In fact, success without God is no success at all; it is an illusion, a mirage and a sweet poison.

"*Big thinking,
tall thinking is what
makes men big and
causes them to be
successful*"

Chapter Six

THINK POSITIVELY

The strong-willed person who believes he can accomplish his agenda, in whom there is no shadow of pessimism, is inclined to succeed. On the other hand, the person who doubts his own ability, and has no degree of optimism is treading the path of failure and cannot succeed.

Success comes to the one who is mentally prepared for it. Your mental disposition is an indication of where your life is heading. The man who thinks failure and dreams no success is on the road of failure and is bound to achieve nothing. We are what we think we are or rather we become what we think we are.

*"The things that are foremost in our minds determine our actions and decisions. We become like our dominant thought."- **Kevin Baerg***

The child that watches violent movies thinks violence, dreams of it and acts violently. Take heed what you keep your focus on. Focus on the good God has destined for you, in order to manifest it.

> *"Positive thinking is a form of thought, which habitually looks for the best results from the worst condition. It is looking at events with the knowledge that there will be good and bad in life but it is better to emphasize the good, and as you do that, good seems to increase."* - **Norman Vincent Peale.**

Liberate yourself from every form of mediocrity. Do not swallow the hook of mediocrity because it will kill you.

Have a positive self-image. See yourself as God sees you. He sees you as a prince or princess, an heir to the riches of God. See yourself as the man you want to be, begin to talk like that and you will become exactly that. Paint a picture of yourself as succeeding, hold that picture before you, and it will materialise. The sense of sight is a powerful force it affects even reproduction. The things you keep seeing are the very things you reproduce.

The power of sight is a powerful force. What is before you have the power to change you and conform you to its standards. The story of Jacob and his uncle Laban paints a vivid picture of this. In the story, Jacob's wages for keeping the uncle's sheep was varied to his detriment over and over again. Finally, the uncle decided his pay was the spotted sheep in the herd. Realising the ewes hardly brought forth, spotted sheep, Jacob painted the post by which the sheep drank water spotted. As the sheep drank and beheld the spotted painted post, they conceived and brought forth, spotted sheep. Wow!

We know also that by concentration, the chameleon is able change its colour in response to its mood, temperature, health, communication, and light.

If a man knows that he will be the next king, he conducts his life in a very special manner. Somehow, he begins to talk and acts as a king even though he is not yet a king. You can also do same because you are *'royal priesthood, a peculiar people and a chosen generation'*.

Positive self-image is seeing yourself in the light of God's word, knowing your worth and valuing yourself with the right measurement. If you undervalue yourself, you will be bought for nothing.

Place a tag of importance on yourself and let everyone see it!

I once listened to a young man who gave a talk on positive thinking. He said, he always dressed well because he knew he would be a man of high social standing in the future and his position would demand that he dress well. Therefore, he was learning how to dress well. Amazing!

Have the right perspective. Believe in yourself and your goal. Believe God ordained you to fulfil it.

The whole idea of positive thinking is based on the divine principle of faith.

Faith is believing something that is not yet visible. It is, knowing that what is seen is the product of what is not seen.

> *"Now faith is the evidence of things hope for and the substance of things not seen." - **Hebrews 11: 1***

One should have faith also in himself and his mission. Because the person that has faith in his mission or destiny may live in dangers and difficulties, but not only will he survive, but he will sail through them and succeed.

Daniel Bonnie, one of the pioneers of America escaped so many dangers because he believed his mission was to tame the land of America, and he succeeded in doing exactly so. When asked how he made it in the face of the many great challenges he encountered, he responded; *'I was ordained by God to open this wilderness'*.

George Kaitholil wrote of him,

> *"His life was beset with many dangers but he believed in himself. He was convinced that though his job was hard, it was useful, and that divine power was protecting him."*

He said further,
> *"It is good for all of us to have that same belief. It will clear away from us all the idle fears and unnecessary anxieties."*

That is what is called tough-mindedness.

Disraeli, the great English statesman said,

> *"Nurture your mind with great thoughts, for you will never go higher than how you think."*

Big thinking, tall thinking is what makes a person big and causes him to be successful. Reach for the stars; have great goals, have lofty ideas, continue to build castles in the air and very soon you will build pillars to sustain them.

> *"Believe it! High expectations are the key to everything"* - **Sam Walton**

But,

> *"Self distrust is the cause of most of our failings. In the assurance of strength there is strength. And they are the weakest, however strong, who have no faith in themselves or their powers." - **Christian Bovée***

Positive thinking leads to the cultivation of a good self-image which in turn leads to success. Do yourself a favour and keep your mind on positive things.

No wonder Apostle Paul advised,

> *"Finally, brethren, whatever things are true, whatever things are noble, whatever things are just, whatever things are pure, whatever things are lovely, whatever things are of good report, if there is any virtue and if there is anything praiseworthy, meditate on these things." - **Philippians 4: 8***

Without the right mindset, princes become slaves and with the right mindset slaves become kings.

> *"Think good thoughts, and they will quickly become actualized in your outward life in the form of good conditions." - **James Allen***

Think you can, believe you can, and you can.

For,

"If you think you are beaten, you are,
If you think you dare not, you don't
If you'd like to win, but you think you can't
It's almost a cinch you won't!

If you think you'll lose, you've lost,
For out in the world you find
Success begins with the will.
It's all in the state of mind.

If you think you are outclassed, you are.
You've got to think high to rise
You've got to think of yourself before
You can ever win the prize.

For many a race is lost
Before ever a step is run,
And many a coward fails,
Before his work's begun.

Think big and your deeds will grow,
Think small and you'll fall behind,
Think that you can and you'll,
It's all in the state of the mind!"
*- **Unknown.***

"*If you cannot
say what you believe,
it means you do
not really believe
in it*".

Chapter Seven

ORDER YOUR CONVERSATION ARIGHT

I remember my mum used to rehearse again and again to me the fact that we were from a poor family. Many parents have time and time again told their children they are from a poor family, so they need to be careful in life. Many children have been asked to return gifts they genuinely received from benefactors on the grounds that the gifts are expensive, in the name of modesty. Unfortunately, this behaviour pattern develops in us an inferiority complex. We grow up to become shy, timid and indecisive.

When you listen to the conversation in most homes all that you hear is a lecture on how poor the family is. When the child asks for a Christmas toy, he receives a detailed talk on the fact that the father has lost his job and the mother is not working and the things they need for the family. When the child talks about his dreams and ambitions, he is made immediately aware of their lowly state. A proclamation that such dreams and ambitions are the result of wishful thinking because they belong to the privileged ones in the society.

We are always full of negative conversations. This is because we fail to think positively. We feed our mind on the negative aspects of life. When we are confronted with a project our mind quickly tells us why it cannot be possible. We find hundred and one reasons why it cannot work. We go about saying the negative, painting a picture of gloom all over the place. Our hearts are filled with fears and negativity and our mouths voice them out.

> *"A good man, out of the good treasure of his heart, bringeth forth that which is good; and an evil man, out of the evil treasure of his heart, bringeth forth that which is evil; for out of the abundance of the heart his mouth speaketh."* - **Luke 6:45**

The words we speak are full of power. Words are pregnant with power, for in words lie the force of creation, the power to build and to pull down. Words are powerful; indeed, the tongue is a potent instrument, which should not be underestimated.

Stop saying negative things about yourself. Think positive thoughts, confess them with your mouth, and vocalize your dreams.

> *"Words are better and worse than thoughts; they express them; they give them power for good or evil; they start them on an endless flight, for instruction, comfort and blessing, or for injury, sorrow and ruin."*
> *- Tyron Edwards*

The devil does not know how you are feeling until you transmit the information to him by saying it yourself. Stop telling everyone how bad your case is. Human beings have proven over the years that they enjoy listening to others in worse situations than they are. Many of the people you talk to about your fears and worries cannot do anything about it. Also know that many who can help you are not ready to do so. Therefore, stop telling every Tom, Dick and Harry your problems.

> *Use the word impossible with the greatest caution"*
> *- Werner Von Braun*

Say positive things, confess right. The fact may be bad, but the truth is good. The truth is what God says about the situation. Do not think you are losing. The truth is that you are a conqueror. When you keep saying it, it shall come to pass.

"How does God create? He does it with words. The miracle of it is that we are to create with words too! Not only is there a miracle in God's mouth, but there is a miracle in your mouth as well!" - **Keith Butler**

The very moment you say something is impossible, you make it immediately unattainable. Say it is possible, for to him that believes, all things are possible.

"Thou shall decree a thing and it shall be established unto thee; and the light shall shine in thy ways." - **Job 22:28**

"… Let the weak say I am strong." - **Joel 3:10**

In the same vein, let the poor say I am rich.

The tongue has the power to create and to destroy. James the Apostle said, even though it is a small member of the body, it boasts great things.

"Death and life are in the power of the tongue: and they that love it shall eat the fruits thereof." - **Proverbs 18:21**

"Pleasant words are as a honey comb, sweet to the soul, and health to the bones." - **Proverbs 16:24**

"A wholesome tongue is a tree of life…" - **Proverbs 15:4**

To confess right is to exercise your faith. If you cannot say what you believe, it means you do not really believe in it. When you speak words of success, you create an atmosphere of success around you.

Nobody likes the company of someone who is a *'wet blanket'*. Do not sound pessimistic all the time. We tend to enjoy the company of people who sound optimistic, who always look at the good side of things and are always encouraging.

Order your conversation aright. Speak by faith and not by sight. Let your conversation be seasoned with faith. When you do this, you command the host of heaven to your side. You bring God into your situation and the angels of God will work on your behalf.

> *"...and to him that ordereth his conversation aright will I show the salvation of God." - **Psalm 50:23***

The salvation of God is shown to the man who has learnt to speak by faith, who uses the power of his tongue to his own advantage and orders his conversation aright.

"Do not run because
others are running,
what is chasing
them may be your
benefactor".

Chapter Eight

BE IN CONTROL

The young man who is tied to the apron string of his parents is heading for a disaster. Such a man cannot take his own path but needs to depend on others. On the other hand, the world will give way to the man that leads the way and shows the way. Who will paddle his own boat across the waters and take his destiny in his own hands.

Do all you can to determine the race you run and the pace at which you run your course. This is in your domain, it is your responsibility, to be the boss of your life and be in control.

It is easy to be a member, a pew warmer, a follower, and a dependant and to be in the crowd. However, it is in raising one's head above the crowd that one sees what is ahead. It is in being a manager, a leader and an independent person that your fulfilment can become a reality.

"We should strive to be the best we can be and to reach the highest levels we can reach. To do less is to be unfaithful stewards of the life entrusted to us."- **Charles Blake**

Lift your head above the crowd, be your own boss, manager, leader and guide and be your own motivator and inspirer. Do not be swallowed by the crowd; do not get lost in the crowd. Do not be a pebble among the stones but be a gemstone. Be distinct, unique and original.

In this world there is only one person that should be concerned about you. That person is not your father; mother, brother, sister, friend, wife or husband. That person is YOU! Stop leaning on others, for if the one you are leaning on gives way, you are bound to fall and that heavily. Learn to be independent because, you will always be there for yourself. Remember even your most dependable person will not be there forever.

Be in control. Be self-reliant. Know you have all that it takes to make it in this life. You are wonderfully and fearfully made. You have the talents and skills needed to manifest your destiny.

I am convinced that no one should live by the opinion of others. A smile may have behind it the venom of hell and destruction.

"The man who is self- sufficient
Will not depend on the good opinion of others.
If he is liked, he will be glad for it,
If he is not liked, he will be content
To go on living according to his principles
His will be no self- complacent sufficiency….
But rather the steadfast, unperturbed,
unassuming attitude
Which is hard to come by."
- Richard Brandon

The person who is in control of his life is independent. He does not depend on others for his well-being. He knows that at the end of his arm is a hand that is always there to help in every situation and at every time.

If you see yourself as the one ordained to fulfil your destiny then you will surely fulfil it. There is a sort of omnipotence behind the man who believes in this. He is backed by an invincible power. When a man sees he is responsible for something, he takes his time to do it well. See yourself as the one responsible for the manifestation of your destiny.

The greatest asset of man is his will; it is the most important gift God has given unto humanity. God has given you a lifetime opportunity to be the driver of your own life. He remains your strength and light, but you must drive the vehicle of life yourself to your destination.

Do not follow the crowd, be yourself, never imitate blindly, never do something because others are doing it, do not be a duplicate but be an original. Do not run because others are running, what is chasing them may be your benefactor.

Let every man respect you for who you are and if they will not, keep living like yourself. Sooner than later they will respect you.

Friend do not introduce anything into your life just because it is being done by another man. When you want to live like others, you will live like a shadow; you will never be yourself. It does not matter what others think or say of you. Live your life in a way that is true to your yourself and pleasing to the Lord.

In Ecclesiasticus, a Hebrew book of moral proverbs and maxims dating back to the Second Century BC included in the Septuagint Bible, it is written;

"Neither to son, nor to wife, brother nor friend
Give power over yourself during your lifetime
And do not give your property to anyone else

In case you regret

And have to ask for it back

As long as you live

And there is breath in your belly

Do not yield power over your self to any one

Since it is better for your children

To be your suppliants

Than for you to have to look

To the generosity of your children

In all you do

Be the master

And do not spoil the honour

That is rightly yours.

The day your life draws to a close

Is the time to distribute

*Your inheritance."- **Ecclesiasticus 33:20-24***

*"Order calls for
diligence and diligence
is the missing link in the
life of the lazy person".*

Chapter Nine

CREATE ORDER

Without discipline there is confusion and order cannot be maintained. Also, without order life loses its beauty and ingenuity.

Many are the pressures that the world and its systems exert on us. So many forces and attractions are driving man far away from his objectives, goals and ideals. You need an anchor that will establish you on your path. Which will prevent you from being carried away by every wind and doctrine. You must stand your grounds no matter what. You must be purposeful, resolute and determined.

You should create order in your life. If you cannot manage the little that you now have, how can you manage the more that you are praying for? Live a life that is well ordered. The person who has no order in his life, who stays in bed till the sun is up, having no waking up time and no definite plan for his day, will see things happening in and around him despite his sincere efforts. Such a man can hardly reach his goal

Order means a condition in which everything is carefully and neatly arranged in relation to one another. To live an orderly life is to live according to plan. It means you should have a plan for your life, a clear-cut agenda for each and every day and a program for every day, every week, every month and every year. It means knowing what you are to do at each and every particular time.

Order makes the execution of a task less difficult. Imagine a carpenter that does not have a specific place for his tools. He must look everywhere in his shop for his saw or chisel and lift everything in his shop when he needs his hammer. His work will be hampered and delayed, and his success will be limited. On the other hand, a carpenter with a well-arranged shop will do his work more efficiently, because he need not look everywhere for his tools. Indeed, he will be more successful.

"Confusion makes insufficiency more obvious."

- Eastwood Anaba

It has been said of Immanuel Kant, one of Germany's greatest thinkers of being so ordered that people adjusted their watches by his daily routine activities. Friend, I am not saying you should live like a machine. However, order is beautiful; it attracts people and success whiles disorder is ugly and it attracts demons and failure. When the Queen of Sheba visited King Solomon not only did the riches of the king amaze her but also, she was dumbfounded by the order of everything she saw in the palace.

> *"Have you ever stopped to figure out how much work you could do if your tools were arranged on a shelf over you bench rather than neatly stored in a drawer? Don't waste your time figuring out how much you have lost, give your time to finding out how you can re-arrange your desk or bench so that the useless is avoided". -* **Dr. Arnold A. Laird**

In an organisation, promotion comes to the orderly man. This is because the orderly man reduces his task by making it less difficult and in so doing, he becomes efficient and useful to his organisation.

Nonetheless creating order in a confused world is not easy. It takes discipline and self-control. It is only the one that has learned to control his life that understands frugality. Self-control is part of the fruit of the spirit and it is a needed virtue. Learn to put your members under subjection. Be disciplined, for without it there is confusion and order becomes unattainable, making life a mess.

"Orderliness is a very expensive thing to attain yet it is a key to accomplishing much with few resources."
- Eastwood Anaba

Indeed, orderliness is a very expensive thing to attain but without it, resources are wasted, capital go down the drain and effort is exerted for no reward. If you are not privilege with a lot of resources, then the only way to make good use of the little you have is to be orderly.

Order is an indication of success. It is awful how some people keep their room. The very moment you enter their room you are greeted with disorder; everything is wrongly positioned, and the room is a mess. If you cannot keep your small room in order, how can you be a custodian of the wealth and the riches of God?

Some people believe the spirit of God is leading them, so they need no plan for their life. They say, the spirit will lead them. They do things haphazardly, forgetting that the Holy Spirit is a gentle orderly Spirit. Achievement becomes difficult without order. If you run a church or an enterprise without good organisational structures, it will not flourish no matter how anointed or gifted you are. Anointing or skill plus order makes your ministry or enterprise effective.

Order means a careful planning. To be orderly is to live according to plan. It is said, *failure to plan is planning to fail.* The failure to conduct your life in an orderly manner is actually the demonstration of laziness. Living disorderly simply means you are lazy. Order calls for diligence and diligence is the missing link in life of the lazy person.

Be disciplined, live your life in order. Live by principles, rules and regulations. Do not do things anyhow. Learn to be resolute. The man of principles is respected and always sought after.

> *"Let all things be done decently and in order."*
> *- 1 Corinthians 14:40*

Without order life is reduced to a jigsaw puzzle with a missing part and work becomes an impossible undertaking.

"Work is not pleasant;
it is not attractive,
it may be tedious and
messy. But it remains
the only dignified
method of success."

Chapter Ten

COLLECT YOUR SWEAT

Without effort, work and sweat you will die with your destiny still unattained. Your destiny responds to the efforts of your hand. Work is a necessary condition for happy living. It is work which produces life, the product of work is life.

You are pregnant with your destiny and it is time to give birth. When you fail to give birth, chances are that the pregnancy will kill you. Giving birth demands effort, labour and work. When a woman is in labour, she must push hard to save herself and her unborn baby. Failure to do so is tantamount to disaster.

"For as soon as Zion travaileth she brought forth her children." - Isaiah 66:8

It is an irony to see people with lofty ambitions who do not want to sweat. They do not want to travail. The truth is that without work nothing can be achieved. Success is for the one who is not afraid to soil his hands, who is prepared to mill his own grains. Remember, '*as soon as Zion travailed, she brought forth*'. As soon as you travail you shall bring forth. As you work you manifest your destiny

The wise man said,

> *"He that tilleth his land shall be satisfied with bread..." - **Proverbs 12: 11***

Every labour is with a profit. The more you work the more you gain. Put in more effort. Work hard! Hard work they say breaks no bones. Do not forget, it is in tilling your land that you have bread to satisfy your soul.

Paul said,

> *"For ye yourselves know how ye ought to follow us; for we behaved not ourselves disorderly among you.*
>
> *Neither did we eat any man's bread for nothing, but wrought with labour and travail night and day, that we might not be chargeable to any of you.*
>
> *Not because we have not power, but to make ourselves an example unto you to follow us.*
>
> *For even when we were with you, this we commanded you, that <u>if any would not work, neither should he eat</u>.*
>
> *For we hear that there are some that walk among you*

disorderly, working not at all but are busybodies." - 2 Thessalonians 3: 7-11

Do not be a busybody, jumping here and there but doing nothing. The scripture is clear, if any would not work, neither should he eat.

Do not forget that the labourer is worthy of his reward. So long as we remain under the sun, work is the constant factor in the equation of success. When you sow you are bound to reap.

*"While the earth remaineth, seedtime and harvest… shall not cease." - **Genesis 8: 22***

It is very disturbing to see young men who are healthy, strong and energetic with their hands in their bosom expecting help from somewhere. No one can manifest your destiny for you. God designed you with so much power and potential for you to manage His creation and create your own world.

In this age of technological advancement, it seems everything can be accomplished by pressing a button. Do not be deceived, that is not true! The principles of God remain the same. Success is the result of work. In manifesting your destiny there is no easy road. You must toil uphill! In real life you will simply find no button to press. Do not forget, no lasting glory is won without struggle, without work; the exertion of effort.

Nowhere is this truth more pronounced than in the field of church work. In ministry there are no fast foods. Everything must be done meticulously. The ministry work demands effort and a lot of work. Nothing can be substituted for times of prayer and supplications, times of study, evangelism and discipleship. Being a pastor is not for lazy people!

"The faith of Christ offers no buttons to press for quick service." - A.W. Tozer

Work is not pleasant; it is not attractive; it may be tedious and messy. Work may be dirty, but it remains the only dignified method of success.

With the pain of work notwithstanding, work is related to happiness. The one who will succeed loves to work. He derives a kind of satisfaction in his work. To such a person work is happiness. When there is no work to be done, he grows weak and dispirited. The maxim, *'work and happiness'*, holds so much importance in his life. Work brings happiness and true happiness is gotten from working.

"He that goeth forth and weepeth, bearing precious

seed, shall doubtless come again with rejoicing, bringing his sheaves with him."- Psalm 126:6

Nothing is achieved without effort. No one wakes up to find himself great. No mission is accomplished without work. We know that without a vision a person perishes but a vision becomes a mirage when work is not added. Mission is vision plus work.

"A vision without a task makes a visionary; a task without a vision is a drudgery; a vision with a task makes a missionary." - George Deakin

Once upon a time, I heard it said that a young man went to see an old sage, who excelled in wisdom, counsel and supernatural powers. His problem was simple. He wanted to prosper. He claimed he was a farmer but could hardly produce enough to feed himself and his young family. He wanted a charm for prosperity. The wise old man looked at him and said, *'collect your sweat'*. The young man asked how, because he could not understand what the old man meant. The sage asked him to bring a bottle of his sweat the next year by the same time. He was to collect the sweat as he worked on his farm.

The young man went home with a sad countenance. He thought the old man was going to perform some abracadabra but that was not the case. The next day he began his assignment as he worked in his farm. Sooner than later he realised that he needed to work very hard to sweat enough for collection.

At the appointed time, not only was he able to collect a bottle of sweat, he had also harvested more foodstuff than any other farmer had in his village.

Friend collect your sweat. Do not be slothful in business. Your success is in your sweat. Without it your destiny will remain ahead of you. Never forget, *'the height that great men attained and kept was reached while their companions were asleep'.*

> *"So whatever thine hands find doing do it with all thine might..." - **Ecclesiastics 9:10***

One of the most valuable lessons about work is story of the ant recorded in the book of proverbs

> *"Go to the ant, thou sluggard; consider her ways, and be wise,*
>
> *Which have no guide, overseer or ruler,*
>
> *Provideth her food in summer, and gathereth her food in the harvest.*
>
> *How long will thou sleep, O sluggard? When will thou arise out of thine sleep?*

Yet a little sleep, a little folding of the hands to sleep,

*So shall thy poverty come like one that travaileth, and thy want like an armed man." - **Proverbs 6:6-11***

Learn from the ant, get to work before it is too late. These are not times for sleeping. Wake-up young man! Because a little more sleep, a little lazying about and you shall end up a failure and have poverty as your friend.

Be diligent in your business;

*"Seest thou a man diligent in his business? He shall stand before kings; he shall not stand before mean men."- **Proverbs 22:29***

The way to success, greatness or achievement is diligence. The diligent man shall stand before kings and not ordinary men. It means he shall walk in the corridors of power. Resolve today to be diligent. Do not hesitate to roll up your sleeve and work.

Note however that, work becomes boring, stressful, uninteresting and drudgery if it is not done in the pursuit of a vision. You must know what you are working for. Work should not be the physical exertion of energy alone, but rather the expression of one's life, personality, abilities, talents, skills and endowments. It should be an undertaking to find one's destiny and to manifest it.

"*A day of favour
is better than years
of struggle.*"

Chapter Eleven

THE RACE IS NOT TO THE SWIFT

In an athletic race the fastest is the winner. However, in life, experience has taught us that this fact is not always the case. It is important for you to work your way out, to put in effort and activity. It remains true furthermore that activity is the sign of life. Indeed no activity means no life. Nevertheless, the presence of activity alone is not the antidote to the malady of failure.

To work and enjoy the fruit of your labour is a gift from the Lord. Your destiny is of God and it is divine. Though you certainly have a lot to do in fulfilling it, it is necessary to acknowledge the part played by divine providence. It takes both physical and spiritual means to bring it to pass. Your effort is a necessary condition but not the sufficient condition for the manifestation of your destiny. To believe you can do it all by yourself is a deception of the devil and the sin of this age. You need the help of the almighty God. You need His strength, guidance and sustenance.

David said of the Lord,

> *"By thee I have run through a troop; and by my God have I leaped over a wall." - **Psalm 18: 29***

Learn to trust the Lord at all times. The person who depends on God is stronger than his adversaries. It is God that designed your destiny and He knows how to cause it into being. His words are yes and amen. He will do what He says He will do, and no one can stop Him or can say unto Him, what are you doing?.

Because,

> *"God is not a man that He should lie, neither is He the son of man, that He should repent. Hath He said, and shall He not do it Or hath He spoken, and shall He not make it good." - **Numbers 23:19***

God is a tested and a proven phenomenon, so I admonish you to depend on Him. Believe Him and have faith in Him.

> *"Trust in the Lord with all thine heart; and lean not on thine own understanding.*
>
> *In all thy ways acknowledge Him and He shall direct your path." - **Proverbs 3:5-6***

Commit your ways unto the Lord and trust also in Him. To do this, is to pray and prayer is acknowledging that you cannot do it all by your strength. It is an invitation for supernatural help from above. There are so many things one can do to improve his lot and manifest his destiny, but I believe the role of prayer cannot be overemphasised. To pray is to acknowledge that you are but human and cannot do all things by yourself.

> *"For promotion cometh neither from the east, nor from the west, nor from the south.*
>
> *But God is a judge; he putteth down and setteth up another."*- **Psalm 75:6-7**

Do not be worried about your lack of accomplishment. If you have done all that is needed to be done and yet you have achieved nothing, take it easy, relax, and still trust in the Lord and you will see the deliverance of the Lord. There is more to life than the eye can perceive. Let God be on your side, He will fight your battles for you, and you shall have your peace. Understand that a day of favour is better than many years of struggle.

> *"Not by might nor by power but by my spirit sayest the Lord."*- **Zechariah 4:6**

Zerubbabel had a great task. His mission was to build the house of God. But somewhere along the line things became difficult. He wanted to give up. There was discouragement everywhere. However, the Lord spoke unto him saying; his task will be completed not by might or by power. It will take something more than physical strength. It will take the spirit of God, the grace of God. By relying on the grace of God the temple was built.

You see, when you think it is by your strength and might, then you will easily give up. Your destiny is great, so you need a greater strength to manifest it.

> *"So then it is not of him that willeth, nor him that runneth but of God that showeth mercy." - **Romans 9:16***

Learn to access the grace of God through prayer. The prayerful person will succeed where others have failed because he commands the forces of heaven. The host of heaven is on his side. Someone said, *'work as if all depends on you and pray as if all depends on God'*. Anyone that learns to add divinity to his efforts is bound to show his worth.

The preacher said,

> *"I returned and saw under the sun that the race is not to*

*the swift, nor the battle to the strong, neither yet bread to the wise, nor yet riches to men of understanding, nor yet favor to men of skill; but time and chance happeneth to them all". - **Ecclesiastics 9:11**

I pray your time and chance come and that your opportunity shall not delay. You shall make good use of the opportunities that come your way. Consider the following scriptures.

*"No king is saved by the multitude of an host, a mighty man is not delivered by much strength." - **Psalm 33:16**

*"The horse is prepared for the day of battle but safety is from the Lord." - **Proverbs 21:31**

Your efforts plus the help of God is equal to success. Indeed, the race is not to the swift. Anyone that comes to this understanding is delivered from the fear of failure. Knowing that God is on your side is a valuable asset. It brings the peace of God that surpasses every understanding. The one who knows this is bound to succeed, for if he falls, he rises again and bounces back into action. Nothing threatens him. He does not make his life and world complicated. He lives a simple but successful life; which people cannot understand.

One reason why many do not succeed is that they worry too much. To worry is to assume that your success solely depends on you. Therefore, any setback takes the spirit out of your life and sets you on an unsuccessful mental expedition. Whenever you worry you deny yourself the grace of God. It is like saying I am lonely and helpless, but that is a lie from the devil. God is on your side; He will lead you into your destiny and future.

"You cannot
be an island, but
if you try to be one,
you will be insignificant,
rejected and unnoticed."

Chapter Twelve

IRON SHARPENS IRON

In recent developments, we see the merging of great firms, which hitherto operated alone. Organisations all over the world are joining forces to enhance their efficiency and to maximize profit.

Nations all over the world have united into various regional blocks, such as, The European Union and The African Union. They have realised that their voice will be heard clearly and loudly in the world if they speak with one voice. In unity they stand to benefit more especially from world trade. Even the body of Christ has seen the need to work in collaboration and many of the ecclesiastical order are working hard to have one voice that will be strong and piercing. There is strength in coming together.

"One shall chase a thousand but two shall put to flight ten thousand." - Deut.32: 30 (modified)

To be successful and manifest one's destiny is a personal decision. However, no matter how successful one becomes, his success is of no meaning if he is the only person in the world. You cannot live your life in isolation; you cannot be an island because you are not one. If you choose to be one, you will be insignificant, rejected and unnoticed. Hence there is the need to network.

To network is to know your strengths and weaknesses and to agree with another to complement one another. It is to unite. It is a move to be strong, for one plus one is better than one. Certainly, two heads are better than one, and *'one head does not sit in counsel'* says the elders.

In times like this woe is one who is alone. These are days of storms. Strong and mighty winds are blowing. Men, women, young and old are falling. If you are alone there will be no one to lift you up when you fall. You need someone to cheer you up, encourage and comfort you. You need someone to wipe away the tears.

You need a shoulder to lean on. You see God made you in such a way that you could not lean on your own shoulder.

> *"Two are better than one, because they have a good reward for their labor;*
>
> *For if they fall, the one will lift up his fellow. But woe*

to him that is alone when he falleth; for he hath not another to help him up.

Again, if two lie together, then they have heat; but how can one be warm alone?

And if one prevail against him, two shall withstand him; and a threefold cord is not easily broken." - **Ecclesiastics 4: 9-12**

Friend, you need people every day of your life. Your success is meaningless without people and to be successful without people is impossible. Often than not you need someone to talk to, not that you necessarily need something from the person but all you need is a listening ear.

"Man is by nature a social animal." - **Aristotle**

We are social by nature. Thus, you cannot put off your social life because of your *'spirituality'* or the pursuit of your dreams. No matter how spiritual you are you do not live on earth with angels but with human beings. We need each other's support and encouragement. Indeed, man is a social animal. We must be relevant to our society because that is what actually measures our worth. We need to remember the strength of the wolf is in the park.

Check the company you find yourself in. For everyone gradually becomes what he is associated with. A man is known by his friends. Choose your friends carefully; they have the power to influence your life positively or negatively. Your environment determines your production. Even animals respond to this truth.

"For a good self-image, choose your friends and associates carefully" - **Zig Ziglar**

This is very important because,

"Birds of the same feathers flock together."

Your friends are a reflection of your life. If you are good you should not be in bad company. Whatever your friends are, you gradually become that yourself. You cannot say you are a good person in a bad company. Light and darkness cannot co-exist, they do not live together.

"However much we guard ourselves against it, we tend to shape ourselves in the image others have of us. It is not so much the example of theirs we imitate, as the reflection of ourselves in their words." - **Eric Hoffer**

Come out of every clique, herd, association or company that is not adding value to your life. It is even better to be alone than to be in the wrong company. Do not move with people who are myopic and pessimistic, who are not wise but lazy. Vacate the camp of the ignorant and the visionless. Pitch your tent on fertile grounds. Sail with the wind. Move with people who will increase your worth and propel you into your destiny.

*"Iron sharpeneth iron, so a man the countenance of his friend." - **Proverbs 27:17***

If you move with fools you will become foolish and if you move with the wise you will become wise. Move with the wise and you will be wise. Move with the rich and the powerful and chances are that you will also become rich and powerful.

*"He that walketh with wise men shall be wise, but a companion of fools shall be destroyed." - **Proverbs 13:20***

"Make no friendship with an angry man; and with a furious man thou shall not go;

*Lest thou learn his ways, and get a snare for thy soul." - **Proverbs 22:24,25***

On your journey to destiny you will meet many people, some are strategically positioned to guide, lead and strengthen you. Be careful how you deal with them. It does not mean they are going to carry you on their head to your destiny. The mistake of so many people is that they do not even identify the strategic people in their life. It is no sin to ask for help when you are hurting. However, to depend on the good will and opinion of others is no qualification and is to be looked on with scorn.

One very important point in life, where many make the mistake of going into the wrong association, is that of marriage. Unless you have the gift of celibacy, marriage remains one of the greatest events in your life. Like any great event, it has untold consequences. It is a company in which you are to remain till death. Any mistake in this regard will make you deviate tangentially from the mean of your destiny. This is important because your destiny involves your total well-being. Do not enter marriage with anyone who does not believe in you and in your vision. Being with the wrong person is like drinking slow poison, no matter how long you live after drinking it, it will certainly kill you.

Everyone yearns to be independent but to be independent does not mean to be alone. Independence means to be immune to the manipulation of others. True independence brings about a sense of belonging and self worth. This is what one gets when he learns to develop the right relationships and to keep the right company.

The word friend comes from the same root as the word freedom. A genuine friend therefore sets us free to be who we are. A faithful friend affirms your worth. In the presence of such a friend you feel you are the most important person in the whole wide world.

> *"A friend knows your weak-nesses but shows you your strengths; feels your fears but fortifies your faith; sees your anxieties but frees your spirit; recognizes your disabilities but emphasizes your abilities." - **William Arthur Ward***

In fulfilling your destiny there is the need for self-reliance. But self-reliance does not mean divorcing yourself from humanity. There is strength in unity. It is marvellous the sort of things that can be done in the spirit of unity. It is called the *'corporate anointing'*, or team spirit. It is in a team that the best footballer can be seen.

Be independent, be self reliant, but acknowledge the law of association. Use it to your advantage and enjoy the blessings of friendship. The other day, I went to visit one of my mentors at his workplace and I saw a wall hanging with the following inscription:

> *"Instinctively the Great Northern Geese fly thousands of kilometres in perfect formation. Here in lies the secret, formation flying is seventy per cent more successful than flying alone."*

Certainly there is strength and unity!
I heard someone say, *'if you want to go fast, go alone but if you want to go far, go with others'*. Obviously, it does not take a university degree to know that going fast is no guarantee for going far.

"The knowledge and
abilities of the humble
person does not obsess
him, it does not get
into his head."

Chapter Thirteen

THE CATALYST FOR GREATNESS

There is a virtue that the generation of today has relegated to the background, but it attracts heaven's attention and pulls success to the one that loves it and practices it.

In the beatitude, Jesus said,

> *"Blessed are the meek, for thy shall inherit the earth."*
> *- Matthew 5:5*

Many people think to be humble is to be weak. To them the meek lacks spirit and wants to follow than to lead. This assumption is not true; the humble possess a kind of strength that the proud man cannot exhibit. Humility is an important tool in manifesting your destiny. Though it has not been taken seriously it remains the compass of your life.

To be humble does not mean to have an inferiority complex. It does not mean to sleep on the floor when you have been given a bed to sleep on. It does not mean to hide in the crowd. It does not mean to follow whiles you know the way better than anybody else in the team does. It does not mean refusing to take initiative. No! Humility does not mean anything negative.

Humility only means knowing and acknowledging that you are but human. Know that so long as you live in this world you cannot achieve everything all by yourself. It is you knowing that there will always be someone that you must look up to and give respect to. Even if you are the boss, humility requires you to tolerate the views of your subordinates. If you think you are the only one who knows how it should be done, then you are wrong.

*"People with humility don't think less of themselves… they just think about themselves less." - **Ken Blanchard***

The knowledge and abilities of the humble person does not obsess him, it does not get into his head.

The word meek has been wrongly defined over the years. It has been misused and misapplied in our day-to-day encounters to the extent that people do not even want to be called humble.

Robert Schuller renders Matthew 5:5 as,

> *"Blessed are the mighty, the emotionally stable, the educable, the kind hearted, for they shall inherit the earth."*

According to Schuller, the meek is therefore the mighty, the emotionally stable, the educable and the kind-hearted. To be mighty is to exercise power with restrain, to know that real might lies in self-control and discipline.

To be emotionally stable is to develop a divine poise through discipline, to keep your negative impulses in check, to avoid and resist distractions and temptations which will excite and stimulate, but which drain your personal, moral and physical resources.

The educable are teachable, they do not suffer from a know it all attitude and they allow room in their life for growth.

The kind is the one that is sensitive to the plight of others, without which one becomes selfish and arrogant.

The opposite of humility is pride and pride is the genesis of a person's downfall. It is the seed of destruction that grows to become thorns and thistles preventing man from reaching his destination.

"Pride goeth before destruction and a haughty spirit before a fall.

*Better to be of a humble spirit than to divide the spoil with the proud". - **Proverbs 16:18-19***

I find it very disturbing when I come across people who have no reputation and honour and yet are so proud. Such people do not have but go about pretending to have. They pretend they have it all; they live a pretentious life and die slowly from within. There is a Ghanaian proverb, which says, *'when a man pretends, he is dead, we intentionally bury him'*. When you are sick and pretend you are not, chances are that, sooner than later you will die.

Do not confuse being positive with being proud and arrogant. Be careful how you see and evaluate yourself.

*"If you insist on measuring yourself, put the tape around your heart rather than your head. Try measuring your wealth by who you are rather than what you have." - **Carol Trabelle***

It was pride that changed Lucifer into the devil. Since the fall of Lucifer, it has remained the stumbling block that has sent many to their graves prematurely. A man's pride shall surely bring him down.

To be humble is the beginning of one's success. The humble man is the one that will become great. Moses was the greatest leader in his dispensation, but the Bible says there was no man as humble as he was in his age. No wonder he spoke to God mouth to mouth.

*"Before destruction the heart of a man is haughty and before honor is humility." - **Proverbs 18:12***

"…Yea all be subject one to another and be clothed with humility; for God resisteth the proud and giveth grace to the humble.

*Humble yourself therefore under the mighty hand of God, that he may exalt thee in due time." - **1 Peter 5:5-6***

When you are not humble God will stand in the way of your destiny. For God resists the proud. It is hard to kick against the pricks. When God resists you, you are resisted indeed. By humility slaves and servants become kings whiles princes are reduced to vagabonds and failures.

Humble yourself and you shall be exalted!

"Let this mind be in you, which was also in Christ Jesus,

Who, being in the form of God, thought it not robbery

to be equal with God,

But made himself of no reputation, and took upon him the form of a servant, and was made in the likeness of men;

And being found in fashion as a man, he humbled himself and became obedient unto death, even the death of the cross.

Wherefore, God also hath highly exalted him, and given him a name which is above every name,

That at the name of Jesus every knee should bow, of things in heaven, and things in earth, and things under the earth,

*And that every tongue should confess that Jesus Christ is Lord, to the glory of God the father." - **Philippians 2:5-11***

*Failure is only
a stop on the road to
your destiny.*

Chapter Fourteen

DON'T GIVE UP

"Two frogs fell into a can of cream,
or so I've heard it told
The sides of the can were shiny and steep
The cream was deep and cold.
'Oh, what's the use?' said the first
'Tis fate – no help's around
Good – bye my friend. Good – bye, sad world.'
And weeping still he drowned.
But the second of sterner stuff
Dog-paddled in surprise
The while he wiped his creamy eyes
'I'll swim awhile at least,' he said
Or so it has been said
'It wouldn't really help the world
If one more frog is dead'
An hour or two he kicked and swam
Not once did he stop to mutter

But kicked and swam and swam and kicked
Then hopped out via butter."
- Unknown

In life many people have become failures because they were not prepared to go the extra mile. They began well but when faced with the storms of life, they raised their hands in despair. They lack what I call the staying power. When there is trouble their strength fails, because they grow weak.

"If thou faint in the day of adversity, thy strength is small." - Proverbs 24:10

There is a day of adversity for everyone, when things become difficult and the going gets tough. When giving up is reasonable, when weeping and lamentation cannot be restrained. However, it is in the day of calamity and trouble that your strength is put to test. How you perform in this test will make or unmake you.

Think about the frogs in the can, both would have died. However, the second one persisted when it looked certain that they had been sentenced to death. The first one died because it gave up.

Dear one, go on, the name of the game is endurance. No matter how dark the night is, daylight shall surely come. There is always light at the end of the tunnel, but you will remain in darkness if you do not get to the end of the tunnel.

Jesus said,

> *"... He that endureth to the end shall be saved." -* ***Matthew 10:22***

There is no point in giving up, throwing in the towel and resigning to fate. He that refuses to give up in the face of challenges and perseveres shall surely have the victory. Your destiny is your life, if you do not persist in manifesting it, your life becomes void and meaningless.

> *"Passionate persistence without impertinence produces progress." - **Schuller***

The fact that you failed once does not mean you should give up. At least you have learned one way by which it cannot be done. Many of the great men you know or have read about have all failed at a point in their life. Failure is only a stop on the road to success. Do not stay there, it is not a resting place, neither is it the destination, it is only a stop at which you should revitalise your system and energise yourself. It is to remind you that you have not reached your destination yet, but you have covered some grounds and soon and very soon you will finish your course.

Just think about the number of times that a child falls, when it is learning to walk. The child is never disturbed by the fallings. It wants to walk like the older ones, so if it means falling over and over again, it will rise up again and again. The one who wants to walk must be prepared to fall. To walk is to fall and to succeed is to fail.

It was said of Thomas Edison the inventor of the incandescent bulb that he experimented for ten thousand or so times before he succeeded in coming out with his invention. I wonder how many of us can try that many times. When asked how he felt after every failed attempt, he said, *'well, what is important is that I've learnt one more way by which it cannot be done'.*

Some time ago I needed to make an important telephone call at a very remote place, where the telephone lines were nothing to write home about. I tried for more than thirty minutes continuously but to no avail. I gave up when some people also came to the only phone booth available to make calls. When I was just about to go, I remembered an old rhyme we all learned in the formative years of our schooling written by Thomas H. Palmer.

It says,

"Try again,
Tis a lesson you should heed:
Try, try, try again.
If at first you don't succeed,
Try, try, try again."

When the going gets tough, it is the tough that keeps going. When the going becomes easy it may mean you are going downhill. It is only when you are making a headway and are nearing your destination that the journey becomes tough and difficult.

I recited it audibly to myself several times and tried again. To my surprise and relief, the call went through.

Persist; keep at it until there is no strength in you. Tough times do not last forever, but tough people push through. To persist, you must develop an inner strength and you must be tough.

"It is not over until it is over." - Matthew Ashimolowo

It is not over yet, do not give up, the game is not over, there is still some time. You have an advantage because the referee is on your side. Press on, press on and you will score a last-minute goal. The game will not end until you score.

"Brethren I count not myself to have apprehended; but this one thing I do, forgetting those things which are behind and reaching forth unto those things which are before.

*I press towards the mark for the prize of the high calling of God in Christ Jesus." - **Philippians 3:13-14***

If you have tried and did not succeed forget the failure. You should learn to forget the past. Do not brood over the mistakes of the past. Sitting down to weep is not the answer.

<u>When it looks like I've failed</u>

"Lord, are you trying to tell me something?

For,
Failure does not mean I'm a failure,
It does mean I've not yet succeeded.
Failure does not mean I've accomplished nothing,
It does mean I've learnt something.
Failure does not mean I've been a fool,
It does mean I'd enough faith to experiment.
Failure does not mean I've been disgraced.
It does mean I dared to try.
Failure does not mean I don't have it,
It does mean I've something in a different way.

Failure does not mean I'm inferior,
It does mean I'm not perfect.
Failure does not mean I've wasted my time,
It does mean I've an excuse to start over again.
Failure does not mean I should give up,
It does mean I must try harder.
Failure does not mean I'll never make it,
It does mean I need more patience.
Failure does not mean you've abandoned me,
It does mean You must have a better idea".
- John C. Maxwell

There is a popular sticker that reads, *'Do not give up your miracle is on the way'*. So do not give up.

How many good enterprises have been abandoned? How many people have stopped on the way to fulfilling their destinies? All because we fail to endure and persist when it matters most. Many have thrown away their spade just when one more dig and the treasure would have surfaced.

Endurance is the litmus test for success.
Practice makes perfect.

Everything in life is learnt by the application of constant

effort. A lot of people admire the way musicians play their instruments. They wish they could also play to the applause of the congregation. They want to learn how to play the keyboard. After a couple of unsuccessful attempts, they want to try the lead guitar instead thinking it will be easier. They begin and to their discomfort realise that the lead guitar is not any easier than the keyboard. They end up trying their hands on all instruments without mastering any.

There are people who want to do everything. Today, they are this and tomorrow they are that. They never specialise in doing anything. They remain, Jack of all trades master of none. It is easier when you concentrate your efforts on one thing at a time. The elders say, it is only when your urine falls at the same spot that it makes a foam.

Jesus told a story about persistence in Luke 18: 2-5.

It says:

> *"There was in a city a judge, who feared not God, neither regarded man.*
>
> *And there was a widow in that city and she came unto him saying, Avenge me of mine adversary.*
>
> *And he would not for a while but afterwards he said*

within himself, though I fear not God, nor regard man,

Yet because this widow troubleth me, I will avenge her, lest by her continual coming she weary me."

The poor widow got what she needed because she was persistent. When you keep asking you shall receive, when you keep looking you shall find and when you keep knocking on the door it will be opened for you.

Accra Hearts of Oak football club of Ghana has as their motto: *'Never say die until the bones are rotten'*. It was in their eighty-ninth year of existence as a football club that they won their first-ever continental trophy. What you think is dead may still have life in it. No matter how dark your road has been, keep going, the Lord will provide light and very soon you will reach your destination.

For all who like football, the miracle of Istanbul is well remembered. Liverpool FC was three goals down at half time in the UEFA Champions league final against AC Milan. Everyone thought it was over. There were wild jubilations on the streets of Milan. But the truth was that the game was not over. There was another half to play. With great focus and determination Liverpool turned the tide around scoring three goals in a dramatic six-minute spell. Liverpool went on to win the match on penalties. Never give up if the game is not over!

Consider these beautiful lines:

> *"The secret is endurance,*
> *Failure is success turned upside down*
> *Men sometimes know not*
> *When they touch the line*
> *Just when the gold was waiting*
> *For one more dig*
> *How many a man*
> *Has thrown up the spade."*
> *- Unknown*

Abraham Lincoln one of America's greatest statesman and a former president had to struggle through life to achieve his goal. We regard him as one of the world's greatest achievers. However, without persistence and determination nothing would have been heard of him.

Here is a summary of his life.

Difficult childhood.
Less than one year formal schooling
Failed in business.
At age 32 he was defeated for Legislature

At age 33 he failed again in business

At age 34 he was elected to Legislature

At age 35 his fiancée died

At age 38 he was defeated for Speaker

At age 40 he was defeated for Elector

Married, wife a burden at the age of 42

Only one of his 4 sons lived past the age of 18

At 43 years old he was defeated for Congress

At 46 elected to Congress

At 48 defeated for Congress

At 55 defeated for Senate

At 56 defeated for Vice President

At 58 defeated for Senate

And at 60 years old he was elected President of the United States of America.

The story of persistence is a story of patience. No one can endure many failures as Abraham Lincoln did if he is not patient. By persistence patience is developed and by patience the flames of persistence are kept burning.

Without patience persistence becomes meaningless and impossible.

Let me end this section with this short poem.

When your strength fails
And your steps become weak and frail.
When your hope is out of sight
And your faith is long, long gone.
There's only one thing that will keep your steps going.
Determination!
Determination!
It's the line between success and failure.
And many a man has failed to cross this line.

*"The man that says,
'come what may
I will keep digging'
will soon find his
treasure."*

Chapter Fifteen

DYING TO LIVE

The only thing that will cause one to keep asking, seeking and knocking is the value he places on whatever he has been asking, seeking and knocking for. The urgency, with which you seek your pen when you have just thirty minutes to an examination and you cannot find it, is explained by the importance of the pen at that time. At other times you would have stopped after a few unsuccessful attempts. I remember times before in the past, when excellent ideas dropped into my mind, I only wrote them down if I had a pen on me. I did not go any step further to look for a pen if I had none on me.

You will stop trying when you lose sight of the importance of what you are trying to achieve. It is very easy to give up. To stand your grounds in times of difficulty takes a lot more than we are willing to give. It takes a stronger stuff in you. To face ridicule and shame is not easy to handle. To carry on with your mission when it has been reduced to a task and drudgery takes a lot of devotion.

Without passion persistence becomes impossible. If you are not ready to die for what you believe in, then you do not believe in it. Let a man believe so much in his destiny that he is prepared to die for it. Such a man will surely succeed.

Be passionate about your vision. To manifest your destiny, you must be passionate about success.

The man who wants to be successful must live today as if it is his last day on this earth.

To be passionate about something is to put your heart in it. Study a young man who is in love and you will understand what passion means. He will go all out for the woman of his heart. What you are passionate about, you are prepared to die for. Passion means a strong affection. To be passionate is to be aflame and to be possessed by something you cannot do away with.

*"Verily, verily I say unto you, except a corn of wheat fall into the ground it abideth alone but if it die, it bringeth forth much fruit." - **John 12:24***

When there is no dying, there is no resurrection.
Until you have your heart in what you are doing, it is bound to fail in times of adversity. The man that says, come what may I will keep digging will soon find his treasure. Are you prepared to die for what you believe? Put your heart in what you want to achieve. Because the hands will keep doing what the heart believes in. The 'bigness' of a person is determined by the cause for which he is living and the price he is prepared to pay for it.

Paul was so passionate about his calling that he was prepared to die for it. He said, *'we die daily'*. Die to live. When you are passionate about something, you do not care about the opposition. You drive on defiant, defying all odds.

All the men and women who have made it to the world's hall of fame were men and women of passion, who believed in their mission. If they were not, how could they have done all the marvellous things we read about them?

Examine people like, Noah, Abraham and Sarah, Isaac, Jacob, Joseph, Moses, Joshua, David etc. These were men that left a mark on their generation and posterity. The Bible accords them a lot of respect and honour.

These men have found a place in the Bible's hall of fame.

> *"And what shall I more say? For time would fail me, to tell of Gideon, and of Barak, and of Samson, and of Jephthah; of David also and Samuel and of the prophets.*
>
> *Who through faith, subdued kingdoms, wrought righteousness, obtained promises, stopped the mouths of lions,*
>
> *Quenched the violence of fire, escaped the edge of the sword, out of weakness were made strong, became valiant in fight, turned to flight the armies of the aliens"* **- Hebrews 11:32-34**

These are all men of substance, men, from whom, we draw inspiration. They were successful in their calling but first, they were men of passion. Their heart was in what they were doing. David's heart was in his mission, that is why he was able to accomplish so much, he wrote most of the inspiring psalms in the Bible. Put your heart in your vision. Let it be a matter of life or death. Go all out for it. Be prepared to go all out in achieving your goal.

Passion arouses the enthusiasm of a person and enthusiasm lightens the burden of work. It introduces some fun into whatever you are engaged in. It is the substance that takes out the irksome nature from work.

It is the joy derived from doing something that you love. It is a strong feeling of interest or great eagerness. Interest and eagerness to accomplish your task is a needed virtue. When you are enthused about something you easily get it done.

The enthusiasm for something makes you a fanatic of the thing. Just imagine the level that people will go in the name of being a fanatic of a sporting activity.

In life, all of us need to be fanatic about something. Be your own fanatic, for life is a game and you make a winning team all by yourself. Cheer yourself up. Believe so much in your goal, be enthusiastic about it and you will find strength welling up in you like a fountain, strength to overcome all the negativity that will confront you.

By this you will have what it takes to stand defying all odds, literally dying to live, doing your very best to achieve your goal and manifesting your destiny in spite of everything.

"Keep pedalling,
for life is like a bicycle
you will fall when you
stop pedalling".

Chapter Sixteen

LIVING IN FULFILMENT

In the preceding chapters, we examined the instruments needed to manifest your destiny. By the application of these instruments in your quest for greatness you shall surely be great and very great. These instruments have been tried and tested. They have been proven to be the remedy for failure and lack of achievement.

All the virtues and principles enumerated must be seen at work in your life if you want to succeed and show forth your destiny. Leaving some out makes your equation incomplete and your answer cannot be correct. They work hand in hand.

"A false balance is an abomination to the Lord." - Proverbs 11:1

Neglecting some is to your chagrin. You must be balanced. I know, *'except the Lord build the house, they labour but in vain that build it'* and *'that except the Lord keeps the city, the watchman waketh but in vain'*. But I know also that there is wisdom in the age-old saying, *'heaven helps those who help themselves'*. When you put your hands in your bosom, the Lord will not descend and build your house for you.

Now you have all it takes to make it, but you see success is more difficult to manage than failure. Many are used to failure, they have failed time and again, and they have a lot of experience in that. When such people become successful, their success begins to tear them down. Many have failed because they succeeded when they were not ready for it. It is my prayer that your showing forth will not kill you.

Keep Pedalling

The way to succeed is the same way to remain successful. When you think you have arrived and then cease applying the principles expounded above, then you are on the verge of falling. When you stop paddling the boat of your life you will be driven in the direction of the storm.

Keep pedalling; for life is like a bicycle, you will fall when you stop pedalling.

Manifesting your destiny is the same. It is a process; you keep manifesting it till your days are spent. The very moment you stop applying the formula you begin to fall.

Dear friend, the fact that your enterprise is now large, the funds keep coming and business is good, is no guarantee for you to stop exercising yourself in the things that have brought you thus far. Many have fallen because they thought they had reached. Do not be at ease in Zion. Do not give sleep to your eyes. For it was when all men were asleep that the devil came to sow tares among the wheat. When you take things for granted, with your own hands you will sow the seeds of failure in your life.

If you have been married and there is peace within your wall, your spouse is giving you no problem and your in-laws have not become out-laws and there is joy and laughter in your house, then give God the glory. However, you need to remember marriage is a process, it is not a product. You must keep the spirit of the union alive. You do not take your spouse for granted. You do not assume that your spouse knows you love him or her and so you do nothing to show that you indeed love him or her. Love must be exhibited and not taken for granted.

Manifesting your destiny is an on-going process. It ends when you go to be with your maker, which is your ultimate goal. When you stop to show forth you grow dim. The light must keep shining before it can be of use to anybody. Living in your fulfilment means continuously manifesting your destiny.

A Thankful Heart and Praising Lips

There are two important and essential things needed in living in fulfilment. These are a thankful heart and praising lips. There are too many people that are disgruntled in life. They are not grateful for anything.

Friend, you must be grateful unto God for bringing you this far. It has been by His grace and mercy that you have not been consumed. He has held you with His victorious right hand.

When you thank and praise God, it is a sign that you acknowledge His works in your life. The man with a thankful heart and praising lips has his light always shining, because he is connected to the source of light. God is always on his side.

The psalmist says,

> *"But thou art holy, O thou who inhabitest the praises of Israel." - **Psalm 22:3***

It takes thankfulness and praises to live in fulfilment.

As you manifest your destiny every evil will give way, when you appreciate the providence and sustenance of God daily. When you are not thankful, you give room to the devil. It means God will desert your habitation and the devil will take over. Many have lost their miracles because they failed to honour the giver.

It is not by your might that you have come this far. Your achievement is the result of God's goodness. You ought to be grateful. Whether you have reached your destination, or you have just begun your journey, there is the necessity for you to praise God all day long.

It is a natural thing to thank God and give Him praise when all things are going well with you. However, it is in thanking God, when the clouds have covered your horizon that the Lord can depend on you. The real test is to thank God when there is seemingly nothing to thank Him for.

The prophet said,

> *"Though the fig tree shall not blossom, neither shall*

fruit be in the vines; the labor of the olive shall fail, and the fields shall yield no food; the flock shall be cut off from the fold, and there shall be no herd in the stalls.

Yet I will rejoice in the Lord, I will joy in the God of my salvation." - **Habakkuk 3:17,18**

Paul enjoins us to be happy always and to,

"Give thanks in all circumstances..."
1 Thessalonians 5:18

Like king Jehoshaphat and Judah, march into your battle believing and praising God. Praise lifts your eyes off the battle to the victory.

One blessed soul wrote,

"Praise will sweeten and hallow all that it touches. Praise will kindle a new faith. Praise will fan the sparks of your smoldering love into flaming love for God. Praise will start the joybells ringing in your soul, you will soon have all heaven joining in on the chorus and you will have a little touch of heaven in your heart. Praise will pierce through the darkness, dynamite away long standing obstruction, and strike terror in the heart of every Satan."

Thank God for everything, the bad, the good and the ugly. Give thanks in every circumstance.

"For all things work together for good to them that love God, to them who are called according to His purpose." - Romans 8:28

Nathaniel Olson said,

"Don't smile weakly and say, 'I'm not doing too bad under the circumstances' when praise can lift you above the circum-stances!"

If you do not have a thankful heart and praising lips, you cannot live in fulfilment. And you will be prevented from showing forth your destiny.

*"The shortest, surest way to all happiness in this world is to make it a rule to thank God for everything that happens to you, for it is certain that, whatever seemingly calamity comes to you, if you thank and praise God for it, you turn it into a blessing. Could you, therefore, work miracles, you could not do more for yourself than by this thankful spirit, for it needs not a word spoken and turns all that touches into happiness." - **Unknown***

Finally, I admonish you to be strong in the Lord, rejoice always in Him. For the joy of the Lord is your strength.

Remember God is not a man that He should lie, all that He has said about you shall come to pass. He has given you all that you need. Go ahead and Manifest your Destiny.

www.ingramcontent.com/pod-product-compliance
Lightning Source LLC
Chambersburg PA
CBHW030322160726
47992CB00005B/2125